CYCLING

A Beginner's Guide

Priya Shah

Cycling: A Beginner's Guide is also available in accessible formats for people with any degree of visual impairment. The large print edition and e-book (with accessibility features enabled) are available from Need2Know. Please let us know if there are any special features you require and we will do our best to accommodate your needs.

First published in Great Britain in 2012 by
Need2Know
Remus House
Coltsfoot Drive
Peterborough
PE2 9BF
Telephone 01733 898103
Fax 01733 313524
www.need2knowbooks.co.uk

Contents

Introduction

If you have developed an interest in cycling and want to learn more about how to get started, this is the book for you! It has been written with the beginner cyclist in mind who may be keen to learn more about different types of bikes and equipment, who wants to discover how to find cycling clubs in their local area or is interested in learning how to protect themselves from injuries while cycling.

There is no shame in wanting to get information on a new activity before you go all out and try to do it yourself. Take the time to read all the information and advice compiled in this essential guide to avoid looking like a novice and making mistakes that could lead to injury.

Cycling is becoming a very popular activity. For the last couple of years, many individuals have expressed an interest in cycling not only to discover a new passion but also to lose weight and become fit. In particular, following Britain's amazing success at the 2012 Olympic Games in London, cycling as a sport and hobby has received greatly increased interest, with a huge increase reported in sales of bikes and cycling club memberships. Whatever the reason may be, you'll quickly discover that cycling has many benefits for your health and also for your wellbeing. Cycling will allow you to take some time off to care for yourself, discover nature and breathe some well-deserved fresh air. Cycling may also allow you to connect with other like-minded individuals looking to form a team, organise events or maybe train for a local competition. You can decide to ride your bike on your own or participate in social activities – you can also decide to ride casually or engage in more extreme riding through the mountains or the wilderness; the world is your oyster!

In the following chapters, you'll discover everything you need to know to get started, beginning with an introduction to the different forms of cycling and the bikes used for each particular one. You'll then learn more about the various accessories you can purchase as well as the necessary equipment you'll need to get started. Other topics covered include common injuries for beginner cyclists, knowing and understanding the various parts of your bike, cycling etiquette when riding in populated areas, how to recognise your progress, staying motivated, etc. For the more seasoned rider, there's valuable information on how to avoid injuries and uselful advice on how to train properly by establishing good training habits, eating properly and making sure that you get all the rest you need to recharge your body's battery after a high-intensity workout.

Please keep in mind that, as with any kind of physical activity, you should be careful at all times. It is easy to get injured or get into an accident – especially if you are riding around town or where motorists may be sharing the road with you. Make sure to wear proper protection equipment at all times and be aware of your surroundings and the proper rules of the road.

On that note, read on and enjoy your newfound cycling passion!

Chapter One

Pedal Power: Different Types of Bikes

Just like there are many reasons to pick up a bike and go for a ride, there are also many types of bikes that can be used. For newcomers to the sport, the different types of cycling and various models of bikes with their different uses and purposes offered on the market can be quite confusing! The five main types of bikes that will be discussed, along with their popular uses, are mountain bikes, race bikes, road bikes, stationary bikes and tandem bikes.

Mountain bikes

Mountain bikes are usually used to ride in the wilderness – this is certainly not for the faint of heart. While you may be avoiding traffic and pollution by travelling the road less taken, you'll also have to battle the elements and equip yourself with a bike that will be comfortable and easy to manoeuver in these conditions. Many individuals will choose something along the lines of a hybrid, trekking or touring bike for this kind of activity.

Just like with everything else, the specific type of mountain bike you'll want to get will depend on the exact type of off-road riding you're planning on doing. Certain cyclists prefer to focus on location and will be happy riding man-made routes in a forest, while others just want to get lost in nature and go where no paths have been carved previously.

Mountain bikes are also used in competitive events such as cross-country, downhill and dual slalom rides.

Popular mountain bike brands include:

'Just like there are many reasons to pick up a bike and go for a ride, there are also many types of bikes that can be used.'

- Kona
- Specialized
- Giant
- Rayleigh
- Mongoose
- Diamondback

There are many brands avaliable and you can select the best one for you based on your budget and riding style. See the help list for details of places you can buy moutain bikes where you'll receive guidance on which make and model will best suit your purpose.

Cost

Mountain bikes can cost from as little as £50 or £60, however bikes priced as low as this are considered an inferior type of mountain bike, known as ATBs. They are stocked by supermarkets and various high street stores and sold through catalogues, and the quality is renowned as being low and some are considered dangerous due to the fact most require self-assembly and haven't been constructed by experts. Realistically it is recommended you should pay between £200-£300 for a bike truly worthy of off-road riding.

Race bikes

Race bikes are most often used yes, you've guessed it, during races! There are different kinds of bike races all around Britain and you'll notice that those cyclists are always very well equipped when it comes to their bikes and accessories. Cycle races are usually quite long, longer than most other types of competitions, and while your equipment is important, your physical endurance and ability will play the biggest part in whether you can be a successful racer or not.

There are a few different types of bike races:

- Road race – A long race, usually lasting several hours, going from place to place. In Britain, road races usually take place on a planned circuit since there is an obvious lack of suitable roads for bike races.

- Criterium – A shorter race presented on a tight circuit (a town centre, for example).

- Time-trials – Very popular in Britain, time-trials are races during which riders are set off at various intervals. These races can be raced alone or in teams depending on the event.

- Stage race – This type of race usually takes place over several days – even weeks sometimes – and includes road races along with time-trials.

Different brands of race bike include:

- Rayleigh

- Vittesse

- Barracuda

- Viking

- Specialized

Road bikes

So far, the bikes we've seen are mostly used by the thrill-seekers who prefer to ride unbeaten paths or ride at phenomenal speeds. But fear not, there are also bikes made especially for individuals wishing to combine fitness with speed and stamina. Road bikes are usually recommended for 'fitness riding', which is essentially the activity of riding your bike for general purposes, usually on the road. Fitness riding can be a solitary activity just as it can be done in groups – you might want to join a cycling group (whether sociable or competitive) to get in touch with other like-minded individuals or just ride by yourself and enjoy the scenery. The term 'road bike' basically describes any type of bike primarily used on paved roads, as opposed to bikes such as mountain bikes which are purpose built for off-road use.

There are several variations of road bikes, including:

- Touring bicycles – Designed for touring, they are robust and confortable and also capable of carrying heavy loads.

- Hybrid bicycles – Designed for a variety of recreational and utility purposes, such as shopping and commuting.

- Vintage road bicycles – These are old style bikes, popular with many who view them as practical, repairable and durable. Certain types often become collectors' items.

- Flat bar road bicycles – Also called a 'fitness bike', mostly used for commuting and fitness riding.

Two popular reasons for using a road bike are discussed below.

Transport

'Cycling as a means of transportation can help you stay fit and enhance your health.'

This is perhaps one of the most important kinds of cycling; it can help you get to work, run your errands or get to school without causing pollution, whilst also helping you to achieve a great level of fitness of health. Cycling as a means of transportation can help you stay fit and enhance your health like no other activity can. No special equipment is needed as you can wear any clothes you like and you probably don't need a special bike to run your local errands. However, there are a few instances where you might need to spend a bit more on your bike and its accessories, such as:

- Long-distance commuting – If you live quite far from work, you might want to invest in nice cycling clothes to avoid having to shower once at work, or a sporty touring bike to make sure your ride goes smoothly.

- Shopping – Running one or two errands should be no problem, but if you're planning on going grocery shopping on your bike, you'll have to get yourself a pannier, trailer or maybe a work bike.

- School run – To make sure everyone gets to school on time, avoid the traffic and use your bike! Make sure to get child seats, trailers or even a tandem bike if the kids are old enough to pedal along.

Need2Know

Recreation

You can also enjoy cycling just for the fun of it. Using your bike, you'll be able to discover new surroundings and escape the hustle and bustle of your daily life while smelling fresh air and getting a workout. Again, there are groups and associations that you can join if you are looking to make cycling a more sociable experience but no matter what the reason, your bike is not only a means of transportation – it can also be a hobby. Two different methods of recreational cycling are:

- Day riding – Usually lasting an hour, or even a full day, a day ride doesn't require any particular preparation. You can go alone or with friends or family, stay in town or explore the rural landscape.
- Touring – Touring is more demanding than day riding, as you'll be gone for extended periods of time. It's a great way to travel, but it also requires a lot of preparation and planning.

Popular brands of road bike include:

- Cannondale
- Raleigh
- Specialized

'You can also enjoy cycling just for the fun of it.'

Cost

Basic road bikes, such as Hybrids, can be purchased for around £100, but for a good one you can expect to pay about £250.

Stationary bikes (exercise bikes)

While some of the more hardcore cyclists may not see stationary biking as being 'real cycling', more and more individuals are getting into this activity and taking advantage of the workout it provides while staying indoors – also, you don't need special clothes, particular accessories or anything fancy to use your stationary bike.

You can certainly find a stationary bike at any local gym, but you can also get one of your own to pedal while watching your favourite morning television show or supervising the kids while they are playing. There are a lot of different advantages to use a stationary bike:

- You can use it no matter what the weather is like. While you can't really enjoy an outside bike ride when it's raining all day, your stationary bike will be there and ready to go no matter how cold, rainy or humid it is outside.

- It's easier on the joints than traditional cycling, so individuals with back, knee or joint problems can still benefit from the activity.

- It's easy to use. There is very little maintenance to take care of and you don't have to grease the chain and clean it up after a day of riding outside.

- You can adjust it to fit your own cardio and fitness level. Most stationary bikes come with a knob to adjust the difficulty and tension of the pedals, so you can take it easy or work extra hard, e.g. as if you are going up a very steep hill.

- It can push you to do more exercise than you normally would. Since you can park the bike in front of the television and pedal away, you might find yourself sitting less and less on your couch and actually enjoying the workout. Because it is readily available and can be used in conjunction with various activities, a stationary bike can help more sedentary individuals discover the benefits of regular exercise.

- Injuries are not as common. You can't get hit by a car, ride into a lamp post or fall from your stationary bike, making it a low-risk fitness activity.

- If you are preparing for a race or tournament, your stationary bike can help you complement your training by allowing you to ride later at night if you get home from work too late to go training outside.

Cost

As with mountain bikes, price can play a big part in determining the quality of an exercise bike. They are widely available and are priced on average between £50 and £500 depending on make and model.

Tandem bikes

Tandem bikes are a great activity if you prefer to ride with someone. A tandem bicycle has two sets of pedals, two seats and two handlebars, allowing two people to ride the same bicycle at the same time. It has been popularised as a great outdoor activity for couples, however you can ride a tandem with your child, best friend or anyone else.

Tandem biking has also gained a great amount of popularity with disabled individuals. Individuals with impairments such as blindness, deafness, etc. can now enjoy the benefits of cycling while riding with an experienced cyclist up front to help them stay safe.

Cost and size

One of the more expensive types of bike, for a good-quality tandem bike you can expect to pay around £800. Tandems are available in a range of sizes, and to get the best out of each ride it is vital you get the right size that is comfortable for both riders.

Summing Up

- There are different kinds of cycling for different individuals, depending on your goals and your interests.

- For each type of cycling, there is a specific type of bike that is recommended.

- The five main types of bikes are mountain bikes, race bikes, road bikes, stationary bikes and tandem bikes.

- Mountain bikes are usually used by individuals wishing to ride with nature and explore the road less travelled.

- Race bikes are used by individuals who wish to push the limits of speed and participate in races and biking events.

- Road bikes are used by most individuals to travel from point A to point B, run errands and ride locally. Accessories such as panniers, trailers and child seats can facilitate many activities such as shopping, taking children to school and grocery shopping.

- Stationary bikes, while not really considered by hardcore cyclists as being real bicycles, are a great way to enjoy the benefits of cycling indoors without subjecting yourself to any risks such as accidents involving cars.

- Tandem bikes are ideal for couples or individuals who wish to ride a bicycle together rather than separately. These bikes have also been recommended for disabled individuals who are not able to safely ride a bicycle on their own.

Chapter Two

Cycling Equipment

Get equipped

If you are serious about getting into cycling and want to make sure that you are ready to go for your first ride, you'll probably want to invest in a few items. While it is entirely possible to enjoy cycling activities without fancy gear and clothing – especially if you prefer to quietly ride around your neighborhood – there are still certain items that are necessary to ensure your safety and protection.

Helmets

Whether you want to enjoy cycling as leisure or have signed up to train for a race, wearing a helmet is a must. Why? Because if you fall, or come into contact with an obstacle, the helmet will absorb the shock, rather than your head. Kids and adults are highly encouraged to wear bike helmets at all times while riding to prevent any life-threatening injuries.

In order to offer the best protection, helmets are subjected to rigorous testing to ensure they meet specific manufacturing standards. However, it is important to remember that these tests can still not fully replicate the serious crashes and collisions that may occur, in a realistic manner.

Here are a few things to consider when buying a bike helmet:

Safety

Make sure that the helmet is safe. To ensure the best level of safety, only buy a helmet that has a CE mark and one of the following standards:

'Wearing a helmet is a must.'

- BS EN 1078 (European standard)
- SNELL certified (B. 95)
- BS6863: 1989

Do not use a helmet marked BS EN1080:1997, these are not suitable for use as cycle helmets. For more information on helmet safety see www.cyclesolutions.co.uk or www.satra.co.uk.

Fit

Try it out and make sure it fits well enough. It should fit snugly and you shouldn't be able to move the helmet for more than one inch in all directions. Remember that not all heads are shaped the same way, so it might be difficult for you to find a helmet that fits perfectly. This is exactly why many manufacturers also offer cushion pads, often secured with Velcro, that you can add inside your helmet to ensure a better fit.

Vision

Make sure that the straps do not obstruct your vision. You need to be able to look all around, so the helmet you select should allow you to do just that.

Clothing

Many serious cyclists will end up investing in comfortable specialised clothing. Following is some information about common items you may want to consider:

Bike shorts

Bike shorts often come with added padding, which will help you stay comfortable through the longest rides. While they're certainly no fashion statement, keep in mind that your comfort is more important than your look! The tight-fitting materials used for bike shorts – generally spandex or Lycra – help reduce air resistance, increase breathability and will help you move around more comfortably. Bike shorts come in a variety of designs, styles, length, colours, etc. There is no general rule, as you can choose whichever style you prefer – just make sure that they fit well and fall within your budget. You'll have to try on different pairs to find the ones that fit you best and are the most comfortable, so make sure to spend enough time at the shop so that you can make a wise choice. Since good and durable bike shorts can cost quite a bit, you'll want to make sure that your investment is the right one.

Reflector vest

If you tend to ride late at night or early in the morning, make sure that motorists can easily see you. Wearing a reflector vest will help you make your presence known. These usually come in bright lime or orange colours with reflector material. If you want to be less subtle but still be safe in darker conditions, choose bright T-shirts or even white clothing for your torso – white will reflect the cars' lights well enough to make you fully visible.

Gloves

These can be very helpful on a cold and rainy day. If you plan on going cycling in extreme weather, make sure to take a pair of gloves with you to protect your hands. You might also want to consider a woolly hat if it's really cold outside, and a poncho if it's raining!

The only way to fully enjoy your bike ride is to make sure that you are equipped properly. Choose comfortable clothing and make sure that you are dressed appropriately for the cold (or warm) weather.

Shoes

Shoes are also a very important part of your cycling gear. Of course, it is very common to notice individuals biking in flip-flops and sandals during the summertime, but let's be realistic; you could really injure yourself doing so. If you are serious about cycling and your safety, you'll want to make sure that your feet are protected as much as possible, while being comfortable for long rides. An unprotected foot could easily get injured during a fall or simply get caught in the chain of your bike – even if you are just riding around town on a

'Shoes are also a very important part of your cycling gear.'

warm summer day, it is advisable to wear trainers. If you are cycling as a fun activity and not particularly interested in specialised clothing, a good pair of trainers will be more than enough.

Of course, if you want to ensure optimal protection of your feet, you could look into specialised footwear for cyclists. You will also need to get a good pair of socks to absorb moisture and prevent uncomfortable blistering.

Road cycling shoes

These are the most common types of specialised shoes. They are ideal for individuals training for a race or cycling event, or even the ones who just enjoy riding their bike consistently on a daily basis. Road cycling shoes feature a rigid and smooth sole to help energy transfer on the pedals. For optimal performance, you'll want to look for shoes that are as light as possible whilst maintaining rigidity. Remember that these are not made for walking and should be taken off as soon as you are done.

Touring bike shoes

If, on the other hand, you aren't training but prefer to ride while still being able to stop and walk around in your shoes, you'll want to get a pair of touring bike shoes. They are less rigid than the aforementioned road cycling shoes so you'll get all the benefits of specialised footwear while still being able to walk around in them.

Mountain biking shoes

These may be small and very light, but they are usually the sturdiest kind of biking footwear. They feature studs on the sole, which will help you to manage all kinds of terrain, and are usually waterproof. Mountain biking shoes should also be comfortable enough for you to walk in, in case you need to; since you'll be using them to ride through rough terrains, you need to be prepared in case your bike breaks, or you get into an accident.

Spinning shoes

These are a relatively new arrival on the market. If you are using a stationary bike and practising spinning, these shoes are ideal for you! They are a sort of hybrid between touring and road cycling shoes – they can be worn indoors and are usually very light, on top of helping your feet stay cool.

Shoes with clips

One thing to remember, when it comes to cycling shoes, is that many cyclists use shoes that 'clip' on to the pedals. If this is your thing, you need to make sure that the shoes you buy will correspond to the latches on your pedals, or that you have the possibility of switching out the clips on the shoes. Please keep in mind that this type of cycling footwear can be dangerous, as you do not have full control in case of an accident, but they are ideal if you are racing or travelling long distances without the need to stop.

Other biking accessories

- Eye protection – Your eyes need to be protected from the sun, wind and any debris that can get in your eyes (bugs, sand, etc). Shatter-resistant sunglasses can help you protect your eyes properly while still offering you great visibility.

- Cycling gloves – These were mentioned previously, but are important enough to be repeated. If it's cold out, your hands will freeze, so you need to wear gloves if you are going to go out cycling in cold weather. Cycling gloves also come with padding, which can help you stay comfortable and prevent blisters even after hours of riding, as well as protect you in case of a fall.

- Cycling jerseys – specialised jerseys will offer you advantages that a simple jumper does not. They usually feature back pockets to store essentials and are longer in the back than in the front to fit well while you are sitting on your bike.

- Saddle – A comfortable saddle is highly recommended. Whether you plan on riding casually or racing, you'll want to be as comfortable as possible when sitting on your bike. You also need to make sure that your seat is aligned correctly and set at the right height for optimal performance and comfort.

- Lock – Sadly, a neccessity in today's society. Securing your bike will deter thieves, hopefully, and if you're planning to insure your new investment your policy will undoubtedly stipulate you must use one.

- Puncture repair kit – Punctures are an unavoidable part of cycling so purchasing a repair kit is a wise idea.

- Pump – There's little point having the means to repair a puncture, but no way of pumping up the tyre after. Pumps, like puncture repair kits, are relatively cheap to buy and can prove to be an invaluable accessory.

- Lights – These are a legal requirement. There are many varieties available at differing costs.

Summing Up

- Being properly equipped will help you enjoy cycling even more. Whether you are a casual rider or plan on racing or doing extreme cycling, you'll need to make sure that you have all the right gear to be comfortable and protected.

- Wearing a cycling helmet is essential to your safety. Helmets are manufactured to help prevent life-threatening injuries in case of a fall or collision. Do not wear a damaged helmet as it will not be as secure. Try out various helmets and make sure that you buy one that fits properly and allows maximum visibility.

- Many companies now offer specialised cycling clothing to ensure maximum comfort while riding. Bike shorts are often recommended for serious riders as they usually feature thick padding on the bottom, which is ideal for longer rides and intense training.

- Wearing sensible shoes is essential when riding a bike. Unprotected feet can get seriously injured and it is always recommended to wear trainers while cycling. You can also purchase specialised footwear depending on the type of cycling you are planning to do.

- Other important equipment includes gloves, eyewear, saddles, etc.

Chapter Three

Challenges to the Body and Mind

As you begin your journey in cycling, you'll most likely experience common hurdles and challenges which are faced by many beginners. Fear not, these will be addressed in this chapter. Cycling is like any other physical activity – it will be hard at first but with some perseverance and by following the advice and guidance in this book, you will be on your way to becoming a seasoned cyclist sooner rather than later.

Sore muscles

Once you've started to ride your bike more frequently, you'll probably start noticing certain aches and pains. While it can often be blamed on poor equipment – for beginners, improper posture, a weak core and other causes can also be blamed for your sore muscles. There are some common aches and pains that you may notice as you start riding more and more.

Nerve conditions

The nerves of your feet will probably suffer considerably at first. Feet contain a wide variety of nerves and these can be compressed or even irritated by the pedalling movement you'll be doing while riding your bike. For example, you could develop Morton's neuroma – a condition leading to pain, tingling and numbness in the foot – or even tarsal tunnel syndrome, which is defined by a compressed nerve in the ankle going through the foot. You could also develop peripheral neuritis – an inflammation or swelling of the nerves. These conditions are often developed by cyclists because pedalling involves repetitive pressure on the bottom of the foot, which can pinch and irritate nerves and other parts of the feet.

Circulation

Cyclists are also prone to chronic compartment syndrome, a condition characterised by increased pressure due to thickening of the tissues or swelling of the muscles. Chronic compartment syndrome can appear as a one-time occurrence or be diagnosed as a chronic condition and is often caused by continual exercise. Athletes engaging in repetitive activities, such as cycling, are more at risk.

Overuse

Overuse injuries are common causes of foot pain associated with cycling. For example, metatarsalgia – which features pain and inflammation in the ball of the foot – can be caused by the use of ill-fitting shoes. Other overuse injuries experienced by cyclists include plantar fasciitis and Achilles tendonitis, amongst others.

Elbow soreness

Many cyclists complain of elbow soreness after long rides or rides on uneven terrain. This is most often caused by bad posture, amongst other things. This is usually not cause for concern, although it is still recommended to consult a medical professional for this type of soreness as well.

Taking care of aches and pains

Because you only have one body to live with, it is of the utmost importance to take great care of it. If you notice any particular pain, ache or think you might be having symptoms related to any of the aforementioned conditions, please consult a health professional in order to address your concerns. While it may be nothing, it's better to catch a condition early on before it gets worse.

More often than not, you'll be asked to stop cycling if you've developed a condition that is quite serious. You'll be instructed to rest and in certain cases you'll be asked to undergo physical therapy to strengthen the affected area and help your recovery.

Posture

Having good posture while sitting on your bicycle can help you minimise the risk of injuries related to cycling. You should keep your back straight while leaning slightly forward to create a slight bend at your elbows. Your biceps and triceps should be supporting your body weight.

Slow weight loss

You may be tempted to start cycling in an effort to lose weight – which is certainly a great commitment to your health! However, many people start riding their bike day after day and struggle to notice drastic changes in their weight or figure.

Beginner cyclists should be aware that biking will help you lose weight but that the process will be gradual and you should not expect miracles overnight. Many overweight individuals who started cycling consistently have reported very little weight loss at the beginning, but you shouldn't get discouraged. Over time you'll start noticing changes in your body and your body mass index will reach a healthy level eventually. However, cycling is not a miracle cure, the positive effects will be noticed in due time.

Slow weight loss, however, is noted to be the best way to lose weight. Individuals who lose a great amount of weight at once often struggle to keep the weight off, while others who slowly but surely shed the pounds are more likely to modify their lifestyle as they lose the weight and make a positive change in their life that will help them keep the weight off and even keep losing it gradually. A sustained weight loss is highly recommended, which is another reason why cycling is good for your health and your body.

'Having good posture while sitting on your bicycle can help you minimise the risk of injuries related to cycling.'

If you are taking up cycling in an effort to get active and lose weight, it is also recommended to use a stationary bike, as you will minimise joint impact. Depending on your starting weight, a low-impact exercise may be more recommended. In due time, you'll be able to ride around outside.

Slow progress

Just like weight loss is rather slow at first, so too can the progress be in the length of your rides, your ability to handle hills, etc. At first, you'll probably progress quite slowly which can quickly lead to discouragement. For anyone who's ever worked out in the past but gave up, discouragement is usually the reason why you stopped exercising; you didn't see the progress you were expecting and just gave up on the idea.

Three scenarios are most likely to happen:

- You won't see any results.

- You'll see results, only to realise that your progress is slowing down.

- You'll progress for a while and then suddenly hit a plateau.

All three scenarios can be rather discouraging, however staying consistent in your cycling routine will help you overcome these barriers and eventually find satisfaction. This is not meant to discourage you, but rather to put a light at the end of the tunnel and let you know that even if things are rough at first, you will soon become an experienced cyclist! If you are getting discouraged by your slow progress, you should consider connecting with other like-minded individuals. Join a cycling group, a spinning class or get in touch with a local cycling club. This way, you'll make cycling a more social activity and this can greatly help you to stay positive and keep your eyes on the goal rather than getting discouraged with each day that passes.

Insecurity

You might be insecure at first. You don't know where to go, where the nicest tracks are, where to get the best equipment or who to get in touch with to join a team or sign up for a competition.

If you are cycling in town, you might also feel insecure riding around in the traffic and find yourself wishing you were more familiar with the rules of the road.

Do not let this stop you – cycling is all about letting go and enjoying the outdoors while pushing your body to do more. Stay safe and be careful – do some research online to find cycling groups and teams or look for information at your local bike shop. The help list section of this book will help steer you in the right direction as well.

Solitude

For the most part, cycling is a solitary activity. Unless you are actively training with a partner or have joined a training team, you will most likely ride your bike alone. Many individuals quickly complain about feeling lonely and feeling isolated, as this is not a very sociable activity in general.

Seasoned cyclists can relate to this – at the beginning it may seem as though you are all alone and can't connect with anyone. However, the more you ride the more you'll be able to connect with yourself and enjoy the peaceful quietness brought by this activity. Some even refer to it as a type of meditation!

'Cycling is all about letting go and enjoying the outdoors while pushing your body to do more.'

Summing Up

- Just like any new type of hobby or activity you decide to start, cycling will present a set of challenges as you slowly begin to move from beginner cyclist to experienced cyclist.

- Physical conditions are very common with beginner cyclists – you are starting to use your body in new ways and may be prone to foot injuries, circulation problems, overuse injuries and soreness in several parts of your body, such as your elbow.

- Individuals who start cycling in the hope of losing weight may not see drastic results for a while as cycling promotes a healthy, steady weight loss. While this may be discouraging at first, cycling has proven to be a very good remedy to obesity.

- New cyclists may also be discouraged if they can't see results right away. You may still be exhausted after riding for only an hour or two, having a hard time managing steep hills or just feel sore all over even though you've been riding for a while. Your health will increase, you will build your endurance and become a better cyclist as time goes by – do not get discouraged and keep at it.

- Beginners may also feel insecure and feel as though they do not know where to start. If you already have a bicycle, start with what you already have. In due time you'll gain enough experience to know what you are looking for in a bike and be able to buy new equipment with confidence. You'll also have a better idea of how to navigate the streets with traffic and which nature-bound paths are the best to ride on.

- Beginner cyclists may also feel lonely and isolated at first since cycling is more often than not a solitary activity. The trick is to treat your bike rides as a chance to get in touch with yourself and connect with your surroundings. Soon, you'll be craving the solitude brought by cycling!

Chapter Four

The Mechanics of Cycling

Cycling is not only about riding around and smelling fresh air, of course. You'll have to gain a good understanding of your bike; knowing each part and how it works will help you know what to do if something breaks down while you're out and about, and better understand what to look for when you're buying a new bike. In this chapter, you will discover everything you need to know (for now) about gears, tyres, seat adjustment, brakes, shocks and more!

Gears

Gears are an integral part of riding your bicycle around. If you already own a car, you probably know a little bit about what gears are – but let's start from the beginning and explore your bike's gears.

Your bike has both front and back gears:

- Front gears – There are three front gears, in general (large, medium and small). You can switch between these three gears using the shifting mechanism located on your handlebars. The largest gear is ideal for when pedalling is easiest and you go as fast as you can – use this one when you're going downhill or when riding a flat surface, for example. The middle gear is perhaps the one you'll use most often as a beginner; it's a middle ground between the large and the small gear, as you've probably guessed. The small gear is usually used when going uphill, as it allows you to turn the pedals very easily, although it will take you more pedalling to go the same distance.

- Back gears – There are seven back gears, in general. You'll switch from one to another using the second shifting mechanism located on your handlebars. It is recommended to pair the large front gear with back gears 1-3, the medium front gear with back gears 3-5 and the small front gear with back gears 5-7.

The general concept is that you'll want to use the largest front gear and pair it with the smallest back gear that you are comfortable pedalling reasonably fast with. In other words, if you are able to get to a higher front gear while still pedalling fast, do it – however if it starts to get too tough for you to be comfortable, change back to a smaller front gear or go to a larger back gear.

Even if you are just a beginner cyclist, you'll still want to get a multi-gear bike. This allows you to climb hills easily or better manage when the wind is at your back. You'll find your ideal cadence (see the glossary) and what the ideal amount of resistance from the pedals is for you – you should always pedal with the greatest amount of power that you can easily sustain for long periods.

'You should always pedal with the greatest amount of power that you can easily sustain for long periods.'

Tyres

Tyres are not very complicated – however you might have problems if you encounter a flat tyre. In case this happens to you, here are a few steps to follow to repair a flat tyre so that you won't be stranded out in the cold for too long! Of course, this is only useful if you have a patch kit with you, along with a pump and a spare tube. Your local bike equipment shop should be able to provide you with all of this and you should always make sure to carry this with you when you go on a ride or plan on travelling with your bike.

- Step 1 – Let the rest of the air out of the tyre if the initial puncture hasn't done so already, and release the brake cable.

- Step 2 – Take the wheel off. If you have a puncture on your front tyre, you'll have to pop the quick-release and unscrew the wheel from the fork. If the puncture is on your rear tyre, you'll have to take the tyre off by turning your bike upside down and pulling the wheel forward off the chain. In both cases, remove all tyre casing from the rim.

- Step 3 – Pump the tube up and look for the puncture/tear. Use your hand to feel air flow while you pump up the tube. Once you've found the hole, buff the tube using sandpaper or the scraping tool in your patch kit.

- Step 4 – Put fresh glue on the buffed area and let it dry for a few minutes. Once the glue is dried, you'll be able to apply the patch – press firmly into place to ensure optimal bonding.

Of course while these are considered 'easy steps', patching a tyre still isn't the easiest thing to do. Ask for tips and advice at your local bike shop to make sure that you are prepared in the eventuality of a flat tyre.

Seat adjustment

To maintain good posture, sit comfortably and be able to last for longer rides, you'll need to make sure that your seat is properly adjusted.

First and foremost, you'll need to check the height of your saddle. Many people ride their bicycles with a very low saddle, which is not recommended – with a low saddle, your knees are bent more than they should, which can cause injuries and harm to your joints. A low saddle will also make it harder for you to carry your weight on your legs and will make you very uncomfortable when riding. You need to make sure that you are sitting high enough to be comfortable but still have a good powerful leg extension to allow you to use strength when pedalling.

You can't judge the height of your seat simply by sitting on it in the shop, in the garage, or taking a quick ride around the block. You'll probably find yourself adjusting your seat several times, perhaps each time you ride, until you find your optimal seat adjustment that allows for both strength and comfort. There is no scientific formula to find proper seat adjustment so just take your time, make you that you are comfortable and do not hesitate to readjust if you feel that something is not quite right.

Brakes

Of course your brakes are a very important part of your bike – without them you wouldn't be riding safely. Here are a few tips for you to follow to make sure that you don't damage your brakes and know how to use them in an optimal manner.

Going downhill

Don't be tempted to put on the brakes the whole time when going down a hill. This can be very tempting, as you may feel as though you're losing control when going downhill at high speed, however doing this can cause great damage to your brakes and burn out the pads. Brake in spurts if you have to.

Use your rear brake sparingly

This is a bit tricky for beginners, but many professional cyclists will tell you that they mostly use the front brakes to slow down and stop the bike. After some practice, you'll quickly get over the fear of flipping over forward and you'll be braking like a pro.

Shocks

Shocks are mostly used for mountain riders. If you purchase a basic mountain bike, it may or may not come with shocks. However, the more you pay for your mountain bike, the better the shocks. Some may come with only front shocks (hard tails) while others may come with a full suspension set at the front and back (soft tails).

If you are planning on riding rough terrains, make sure that you get a good suspension, as you'll notice quite quickly that it's harder to manoeuver and stay comfortable while riding bumpy roads. Your local bike shop will be able to help you purchase the best suspension for your bike and make sure that you don't pay more than you need to, or buy something that won't really make a difference.

Summing Up

- Knowing the various parts of your bike and how to do minor repairs is an integral part of being a cyclist. Whether you are a beginner or not, you'll get flat tyres, will need to buy new equipment or replace parts on your bike, so you definitely need to be as familiar with your bicycle as possible.

- Understanding how your gears work will help you enjoy cycling even more. Once you get used to switching from one gear to another and understand how the front and rear gears work together, you'll have no problem going uphill, downhill, facing the wind and much more.

- Your bike will normally have three front gears and seven rear gears. You can adjust these in relation to each other to help you use less strength when going uphill or pedal faster when riding flat terrain.

- You should know how to patch a flat tyre in case it happens to you in the middle of nowhere. Make sure to purchase a patch kit at your local bike shop and know how to use it.

- Take care of your brakes and understand how to use them wisely to avoid damage.

- Invest in some good shocks if you are planning on mountain biking. Ask for advice on whether you should get front, rear or full suspension and make sure that you are getting your money's worth when purchasing a mountain bike or just the suspension.

Chapter 5

Precautions and Cycling Injuries

Injuries have been mentioned in the previous chapters, but it's important to realise that even if you're not training for a competition or riding long distances, you could still injure yourself and cause harm to your body while cycling. In this chapter you will discover how to avoid common injuries and stay safe at all times.

Safety precautions

Bicycle checklist

Before going on a ride, always make sure to check your bike thoroughly. You should make sure that the seat, handlebars and the wheels are solidly attached to the frame of the bicycle and that nothing is wiggling around. Make sure that your chains are nicely oiled and greased regularly and that your brakes are in good condition. Make sure that your tyres are fully inflated, leak free and that you have a few reflectors installed to be visible.

Proper gear

You need to ensure that you are well equipped for your ride. Always wear bright clothing to alert others of your presence and make sure that you wear protective sunglasses to prevent debris from obstructing your vision. You should also be careful to tuck in your shoelaces, backpack straps and any other loose part of clothing that could get caught in your chains, pedals, etc. Make sure that you are wearing appropriate footwear.

Safe riding

Basic safety rules apply when you are cycling. Keep both hands on the handlebars at all times and only cross streets at intersections. Always look out for traffic on both sides and be cautious when riding near parked cars as drivers may open their door suddenly and without noticing you. Observe basic traffic rules and watch out for obstacles such as puddles, rocks, wet leaves, etc. You'll learn more about safe riding and how to ride in a group safely in the following chapter.

Cross training

It is important to realise that cycling only works the lower half of your body. In order to stay in great shape and make sure that all your muscles get the workout they need, it is highly encouraged to cross train.

'Cross training simply means to supplement your main workout with activities and exercises targeting different part of your body.'

Cross training simply means to supplement your main workout with activities and exercises targeting different parts of your body. Since we'll assume that cycling is your main workout, you'll need to find ways to supplement this workout by working your upper body. It is also important to note that cross training can also use an activity that works similar muscles as your main workout, or mimic a similar movement, in order to build on that strength and those muscles in a different way. Here are various options to consider for cross training:

Running

This may sound surprising, but running is an excellent option to supplement cycling. While running will be able to enhance your leg strength and help you pedal even faster and harder, it will also help you develop certain upper body muscles. Running is also more demanding cardio-wise than cycling.

Ice skating

The striding motion of skating mimics the leg motions of pedalling, so ice skating is a great way to build on that existing leg strength while involving different muscles, such as your glutes and quadriceps. It is also important to note that skating will offer you the same benefits as running but without the joint impact.

Swimming

Swimming is a great exercise, both for cyclists and non-cyclists. You will be able to develop your cardiovascular fitness while exercising your arms and upper body. It is also a low-impact exercise, which helps prevent any additional injuries.

Elliptical training

Elliptical training also mimics the pedalling movement, while improving your cardiovascular fitness and involving your hips, quads and abdomen. Elliptical trainers (machines) are used to stimulate stair climbing, walking and running without causing excessive pressure to the joints.

Rowing machine

Using a rowing machine to supplement your workout will help you work out your thighs, hips, buttocks, lower and upper back and your shoulders. It will also help you increase your cardiovascular fitness.

Weightlifting

Working out in a weight room can be very beneficial when cross training. Here are a few exercises that will make you stronger:

- Leg press.
- Calf raise.

- Hamstring curl.
- Leg extensions.
- Squats.

Training schedule

If you are serious about cycling and want to start training like a professional, you'll want to start planning an efficient training schedule. The first step to do this is to cut down the time you spend on time-ineffective cycling training. Time-ineffective training is activities you spend a lot of time on for very little results. Some good examples of time-ineffective training are:

- Recovery rides.
- Social rides.
- Long, slow distance training.

Of course, it is not to say that you simply can't go out and enjoy a slow ride with friends and family, but simply that these should not comprise the bulk of your training or workout. High-intensity workouts should be the core of your training sessions and should never be reduced in volume. By reducing time-ineffective workouts, you'll discover many advantages:

- You will be more focused and put more energy in your remaining training sessions. By eliminating activities that are time-consuming and don't offer the same benefits as high-intensity workouts, you'll save yourself for when you really have time and energy to put into your high-intensity workouts and be more focused when training.

- You will become a more competitive athlete. The more you ride at high intensity and high speed, the better you will become and you will gain an edge on other cyclists.

- Riding at a competitive intensity will help you feel more comfortable in pelotons (see the glossary) and you will be more comfortable handling your bike in stressful situations.

- While riding at fast speeds, you brain will be more focused and you will be more concentrated on each and every moment that passes. This can have repercussions on all aspects of your life, as you gain better concentration on every activity you will invest yourself in.

- Your success ratio will dramatically increase if you go out for fewer short training sessions. By training at high intensity, you'll eliminate the need for long training sessions and will spend less time riding endlessly with no results.

Eating right

Riding your bike more often certainly does not give you a free pass to eat whatever you want! This is especially true if you are training for an event. You want to be fit, not sluggish. You will need to make sure that you are consuming enough calories to get you through the day and through your training sessions, but you'll also need to make sure that you are eating right and following a good diet.

Cyclists are encouraged to consume plenty of low fat and high carbohydrate foods. These will help you get the energy you need to pull through your training sessions. You may be surprised to learn that you will need to consume carbs, but these are perhaps one of the most recommended foods for cyclists. While cycling, you are burning carbs to fuel your activity, so you need to make sure that you replace those lost carbs. Of course, you'll also need to consume enough liquids to provide thorough hydration for your body.

Remember also that the time at which you eat is as important as the actual food you eat. Do not eat right before a ride, as this will make you feel very uncomfortable and could cause cramps. However, make sure that you fuel up about an hour before a bike ride. Choose a small meal or high carbohydrate snack. For example, you could choose to consume fresh fruits and wholegrain toast or a bagel with peanut butter. Remember to eat, especially if your ride is more than an hour long. Many researchers have found that refuelling every half hour – beyond the initial hour – with 30 to 40 grams of carbohydrates will help you stay focused, full and healthy.

After your ride, make sure to eat within an hour to replenish your body.

'Your success ratio will dramatically increase if you go out for fewer short training sessions.'

Of course, it will never be said enough that you need to drink plenty of fluids during and after a high-intensity workout. Make sure that you carry sports drinks or plenty of water with you when you are training. Dehydration is very damaging and you need to make sure that you are consuming enough fluids to prevent thirst and dehydration.

Sleeping right

If you are training, not only do you need to plan your training and eat right, but you'll also need to make sure that you are getting all the sleep you need to be efficient, focused and energised. Proper sleep and good sleeping habits will make you stronger and a more competitive cyclist. Many professional athletes will attest to the fact: a good night's sleep will give you an edge on a tired cyclist. If you are planning on racing or participating in events, make sure that you do get a good night's sleep before. Of course, you need to make sure that you get a good amount of sleep every single night for optimal performance on a daily basis.

'You'll also need to consume enough liquids to provide thorough hydration for your body.'

For many people who have families, work and lots of responsibility, getting enough sleep may be quite difficult to achieve. Here are a few tips for you to make sure that you get the rest your body needs:

- If you must eat in the evening, choose your foods wisely. A light snack with dairy, fish, turkey, nuts and beans can actually help you fall asleep, as these ingredients contain tryptophan, a natural sleep agent. Do not consume sweet or fatty food before bed or as an evening snack.

- Sleep following a regular routine. Many researchers have proven over and over again that going to bed at the same time and waking up at the same time every day will help you establish good sleep patterns and condition your body to rest on a regular schedule, which will help you fall asleep and replenish your energy.

- Make sure that you are sleeping in an optimal resting environment. Turn off the lights and turn off all electronics that may make a noise. Make sure that your room is quiet and comfortable.

- Avoid things like caffeine, nicotine and alcohol before bed. Caffeine is a no-brainer, as it will work to stimulate your body and keep you awake.

Nicotine should also be avoided (for many other reasons, especially if you are training for a cycling competition!) and shy away from the late nightcap. Alcohol may give you the impression that you are sleepy at first, but within a few hours the alcohol will act as a stimulant in your body and you might feel restless or lie awake instead of getting the rest you need.

▨ You will also need to make sure that you actually get the time to rest and make it a priority. Don't stay up late to meet some sort of deadline or take care of house chores, and don't plan on waking up earlier to get something done before you start your day. Make sleeping a priority and don't cut your sleeping time for other activities. Schedule yourself a good night of sleep and make sure that you get enough sleep day after day, especially if you are training at high intensity frequently. Sleeping should be part of your workout routine in many ways.

Summing Up

- As a cyclist, you will be prone to injuries and accidents. There are certainly a few things you can do to reduce your chances of these occuring.

- Follow all safety precautions. Make sure that your equipment is in order before you leave for a ride and that you follow basic safety rules when riding your bike.

- You'll also want to consider cross training to make sure that your entire body gets a good workout. Great cross training options include running, swimming, weightlifting, and more.

- If you are planning on training for an event or simply becoming a more competitive cyclist, you'll need to establish a plan for yourself to avoid injuries and accidents. You'll have to work on improving many aspects of your life, including eating and sleeping.

- The first step to efficient training is to plan your training sessions carefully. Eliminate time-inefficient activities such as recovery rides and long slow rides, for example.

- You'll want to develop good eating habits and make sure to consume enough carbohydrates and fluids to replenish all that is lost while you are cycling at high intensity.

- Good sleeping habits are also important. Make sure to establish a good sleeping pattern and schedule, and make sure that you are getting all the sleep you need to properly recover from your training sessions.

Chapter 6

Riding Safely and Cycling Etiquette

Riding safely with motorists

Bicycle etiquette is not exactly like manners at the dinner table because while you may not get dessert for lack of manners, a cyclist's lack of manners may result in a serious accident! Also, demonstrating the proper etiquette may help keep motorists from being angry about sharing the road with cyclists. An inconsiderate cyclist makes it hard for motorists to know how to drive safely near them and that can be frustrating and dangerous. If you keep these four situations in mind and stick to the rules of the road, then you should be riding safely in no time.

Riding with traffic

Many cyclists love to be out on the roads enjoying nice weather and good exercise, but they must be aware of the motorists on the road. Cyclists should *never* ride against traffic. This is important because heading into oncoming traffic is not the expected or accepted method of cycling, so if it happens it can be nerve-racking for the motorist. Unexpected movements by cyclists, for example if they encounter an obstruction on the side of the road cause more problems for motorists if cyclists are coming head on towards them. By riding with the flow of traffic, motorists have plenty of time to see the cyclist and possibly pass, if needed.

Traffic lights and stop signs

Obeying all traffic lights and stop signs is critical to the safety of a cyclist. Any traffic law that a motorist is expected to follow needs to be followed by a cyclist as well, to keep everyone safe. Coming to a full stop at a red light and at a stop sign is expected for cyclists as well as motorists.

Hand signals

Motorists use indicators and brakes that are visible to others behind them. These let others know that they will be turning at the next junction. Cyclists do not have them, but they still need to signal somehow when making a turn. Hand signals are the way that a cyclist can best communicate their intention. That way, the motorist will know what the cyclist will be doing once the light turns green or at the next junction, for example.

Prepare to brake

As a safety precaution, cyclists need to use the brakes at any moment. Keeping both hands on the handlebars of the bicycle lets a cyclist reach the brakes easily. If something unexpectedly pops out in front of a cyclist, being ready to stop in an instant is critical. Using one brake can slow down the braking process and this can create a hazard on the road.

Same rules for all

Using proper cycle etiquette and adhering to the same rules on the road can keep cyclists and motorists alike safe. By being a predictable road mate, cyclists may receive more tolerance from motorists. Drivers will know what to expect from cyclists if they follow the same rules.

Cycle trails

Today there are many cycle trails and routes winding through parks and other green spaces. These are ideal for different activities, like bird watching or spying on wildlife and nature, hiking, walking and running, and cycling, too. Sometimes, you may even see people on horses. With narrow paths and everyone moving at their own pace, the obstacles for cyclists are many and varied. What about those who travel as a group and insist on staying together no matter whom else wants to use the trail? If you add mobile phone and iPod usage, then you have distracted cyclists/pedestrians that can be unaware of others around.

Now, consider that there are intersections on trails with other trails, roads and rest areas. People need to stop at these and may not be aware of how close others are to them when they do. If you travel at high speeds, inclines, bends and curves present obstacles that need quick thinking and reflexes to navigate.

Listening to news reports, obesity is on the rise in the UK, making it sound as though the British are all sedentary and lazy, but if you find yourself on a cycle trail, you will have plenty of company. As mentioned in the introduction, the popularity of cycling is on the rise and maybe such news reports have made more people seek outdoor physical activities. The problem with this amount of people is that congestion occurs. Instead of getting in shape and becoming healthier, some people are taking unnecessary risks that actually put themselves and others at risk.

One problem with all the activities happening on one trail or route is that there are not set areas to travel, like lanes on a road, and the rules seem to be assumed and not learned by all as in driver training for a car. Trail users travelling at different speeds combined with vague or absent trail markings make travelling on a cycle trail as dangerous as being on a road with motor vehicles.

Just as on the roadways, trail safety is something that authorities are attempting to address by perhaps widening the lanes, making markings clear and even adding rumble strips in some well-known high speed areas, all in the hope of keeping the rising accident rate down.

Remember this: Nearly all cycle accidents are preventable.

'Remember this: Nearly all cycle accidents are preventable.'

Top ten rules for safety

1 – There is a right of way hierarchy. Horses first have the right of way, then pedestrians, runners and skaters. Cyclists should yield to all other cycle trail users. Moving in a steady predictable way can avoid startling others and interfering with their outdoor experience. Courtesy is the ultimate prevention method.

2 – Passing others on their left and leaving at least two feet in-between is a safe way to go past somebody. Also, the passer should call loud enough for others to hear, 'Passing on your left.' Make sure that this warning is done in plenty of time before actually reaching that person.

3 – Avoid listening to music so loud that you can't hear others warning you of obstacles or of passing. Consider only listening to music in one ear and leaving the other for noises and warnings of hazards.

4 – Control speed when there is a great deal of congestion on the trail, and respect trail conditions. Cyclists must be aware of speeding through areas where they may encounter something unexpected. Hitting a pedestrian with a speeding bicycle can cause significant injury.

5 – Watch trail signage. These warn of intersections, hills and other potential areas that need extra care in navigating.

6 – Move off the trail. If you stop to see animals, flowers, trees or birds you should be mindful of other trail users. Take pushchairs, bicycles and any gear like helmets from the trail, if you stop.

7 – Move in single file. If there is a group travelling together they must be alert to avoid bothering others or taking over the trail.

8 – Keep pets under control and keep track of small children. Children and pets should be on the right side. Pets should be on a short leash so that they won't get tangled up.

9 – Unless you are in a motorised wheelchair, no motorised vehicles are allowed on trails.

10 – Consider weather conditions. Trails aren't kept clear of snow and ice. Also, heavy rains or flooding can wash out trails or leave debris behind.

Weigh the risks. Be aware of your surroundings, but still enjoy your activities and exercise. Be smart and healthy on the cycle trails and routes.

Riding in a group

Some dos and don'ts:

- If you are riding on the road or even on a trail wearing headphones is not a great idea, but if you are planning on riding in a group, then it definitely isn't advised. Headphones on a group ride can send the wrong message to the others on the ride. First, people may assume that you are not willing to interact with anyone. Also, people may see the headphones as a disregard for their safety and that you are reckless. Neither is a message that you want to convey to the members of your group.

- Wear shoes that are designed for the type of cycling you're doing rather than trainers or mountain bike shoes.

- Be polite! Manners matter especially because the more bad experiences with cyclists, the more motorists will hold a poor attitude towards all cyclists.

- Ring your bell or call out to let pedestrians, roller-bladers and other cyclists know you are coming. Just make sure to do it in time for them to react.

- Communicate to others passing by you. Nod your head, wave and say hello when someone is near. If you are not doing road intervals, take the time to chat with other cyclists for a few minutes.

- Ask before drafting (see the glossary) because the faster person may not like a 'hanger on' and may not appreciate doing more work while you enjoy his energy-saving wake. If you get permission, try to take a turn up front, too. Signalling when slowing down or before changing lanes will keep you from crashing.

- Be thoughtful and move everything off the path if you stop for some reason.

- Encourage younger cyclists. Comment on the cool helmets or for stopping at corners and using other road manners that can keep them developing good habits.

■ Invite others to join you for a ride. If someone is a novice, then make sure you stay with them and help when you can. Offer tips to improve their cycling, but don't brag about your own riding skills. Focus on their riding progress. Be positive and supportive.

Slow rider etiquette

Group riding does have some etiquette to consider as well. A paceline formation is a group ride in which each person takes a turn riding in front and breaking the wind for the rest of the group. The etiquette for this type of cycling is designed to keep the group's speed consistently high and to keep everyone safe and accident-free.

The reason the paceline can help to keep speed high is because it works on the physics that it is nearly thirty percent easier to ride behind someone because the wind resistance is much less.

Avoiding accidents is another reason that paceline is effective. When the wheels of the bicycles are inches apart from one another, accidents can happen.

The essential purpose of a paceline formation is efficiency. If the group ends up with gaps in it, or the front positioned person doesn't seem to give a clear idea of their intentions to move aside and let the next person take over the lead, then the line can be less efficient pushing to close gaps and catch up. If you picture an accordion opening and closing, there are some parts that are closer together and others that are far apart.

What if you are in line and the rider in front of you is now nearly five feet ahead instead of one foot? You need to pedal hard to close the gap as does the rest of the pack behind you. Being clear when to move up to the front when it is your turn is important to the safety and the movement of the pack

Keep these three things in mind when in a paceline:

1 – Keep your speed steady when you assume the front position. Eventually, like the accordion example above, the gap-closing effort wears down the riders. The rider who will become the front rider must watch the speed right

before they assume the position. They must keep that speed when they become the front and if the speed needs to be increased then the time to do it is after a bit in the lead position, and do it slowly.

2 – When you are finished pulling on the front, move off to the side with a crisp, safe movement. Make sure that you are moving in a deliberate way off to the side so that the next person will know that they are the front now.

3 – After you have pulled off of the front, slow down immediately. After moving to the side, you must immediately slow down because the next rider needs to move off the front without bumping into you. Don't make the rider wait for you to get out of the way. Be careful to not back into a rider behind you when you slow down.

With these few guidelines of paceline etiquette you will be in good shape while riding in a group.

Sharing the road

While sharing the road sounds like a great idea, the reality is that it isn't always easy to do. There are some ways to keep yourself safe while cycling, but when they are ignored, then it can mean injury or even death. The majority of cyclist deaths occur between the ages of 15 to 35. Don't be one of those casualties.

Here are some things to keep in mind:

* Ride to see and be seen – wear bright colours and use lights at night.
* Don't use headphones or your phone while riding.
* Ride out from the side of the road to make sure you are seen at intersections and are away from any debris on the side of the road.
* Wear a helmet.
* Be a door's width from a parked car as you pass, so if it opens unexpectedly, then you can keep from being knocked over.
* Obey traffic signals and signs.
* Politely remind others to obey the rules as well.

- Check your bike to make sure the brakes work and the tyres are pumped up.
- Ride close together in parallel lines, when appropriate.
- Keep a foot in length between your shoulders and the rider next to you.
- Ride in single file on busy roads.
- Listen to any calls for movement or caution from others in the line and repeat to others behind you.
- Ride close behind the rider in front of you and stay in line.
- Brake smoothly.
- When you are in the front keep pedalling, even downhill, because if you don't the people behind you will all have to brake.
- Communicate with each other – use hand signals and calls.
- Ask to have the group slow down if you or someone else begins to fall behind.
- Ease up or slow a little by pedalling less hard for a bit or freewheeling.
- Ride at a steady pace.
- Check over your shoulder for other riders or traffic when passing.
- If you are in the front make sure that you call all clear or wait at intersections to make sure that everyone knows what to do to keep safe.
- Let others know if you are tired.
- Dress appropriately for the weather.
- Take everything that you might need like spare tubes and tyre repair kits and a pump.
- Relax and have fun!

Summing Up

- Obey all traffic laws, signs and signals.

- Use hand signals to let motorists know your intentions.

- Be courteous and polite to other riders and encourage younger ones.

- Make sure to ride safely and slower on crowded trails.

- Learn how to ride safely in a group or pack.

- Share the road with motorists and be smart about taking supplies.

- Use riding etiquette so that everyone is safe.

Chapter 7

The Road to Progress

Signs of progress

Cycling is an easy activity to get involved in because in order to get started you need to get into the routine of cycling and build from a short time to longer rides.

Begin with a ten-minute ride that is close to your house. Don't worry about the distance at this point, go for the time. If you need to go around your short route twice to make the ten minutes, that is okay.

Begin your biking with a low resistance or easy pedalling time as a warm-up and end it the same way. This provides a warm-up for your muscles and a cool down before you end your workout.

If you eventually wish to finish your route strong with a sprint, then still allow two minutes or so of relaxed pedalling to cool down. After a strenuous ride make sure to stretch as well.

At the beginning, do at least three days per week with the ten-minute rides for the first two weeks. You should notice your improvement quickly and the ten minutes will begin to feel easy. Write down the distance that you covered with each ride and this can become your base level. (Check an online map to verify distances.)

Now, you can start to progress from your base level. Each week you can increase the time that you cycle just a bit. For example, the first week might be a twelve-minute ride and then the next week a fifteen-minute one. Write down your distances so that you can try to improve with each ride that week.

When you reach thirty minutes for five times per week you are exercising at a healthy level.

Goals and targets

Depending on your goal for the cycling you have some options . . .

If weight loss and being healthy is your goal, continue this progression until you reach your target weight. Cycling thirty to forty-five minutes four or five times per week should help you reach your goal.

If building endurance is what you want, then continue progressing until you can do two sixty-minute rides per week. Include one two-hour rides per week and keep the other shorter rides, too. Gradually work up your endurance. Maybe treat yourself to a forty-mile nature ride every month.

Including sprints in your ride is a good idea in general. Try to do one or two short sprints if you are cycling at least thirty minutes. This helps to increase your strength.

If doing sprints is your goal, then work out for shorter times and strive to improve your speed. Include two ten-minute rides per week in which you go as fast as possible to beat your previous distance. You can also set a distance, like three miles and then try to beat it each time.

Try off-road mountain biking with a group of people as a nice variation of your usual road bike routines. Make sure to go on a recognised trail, so you don't get lost. Be careful!

Once you get into the routine of cycling, varying your exercise workouts from day to day or week to week keeps things interesting and also can offer challenges that you haven't considered until you give something new a try.

Hills and plateaus

Increasing both strength and ability to apply force to the pedals to overcome resistance is something that can be accomplished by climbing short, steep hills or riding into a head wind and even riding in a higher gear.

Having a high level of core strength is an important ability for every cyclist – almost a necessity. If you combine this with your 'pure' endurance for finishing a long ride, you will be able to tackle many different rides and that means enjoying all sorts of group rides, charity ones and even just a longer solo ride.

If you ride where there are hills and windy areas, having enough strength to push a bigger gear on the flats and to crest a short and maybe steep hill, or to battle the head winds comes in handy.

To increase strength, increase the frequency first. If you are riding only a couple of times per week, riding more often can do this. When you do more riding over varied terrain it helps to build strength and is a key to improvement.

This is a first step to increasing both endurance and strength. Once you have started to see some gains, then you can graduate to higher intensity workouts both on and off of the bike.

Joining a cycling club

After a few months of experience in the saddle building your confidence and stamina, you may find yourself wondering, what's next along the route for you? Well, the answer could be – join a cycling club. Like many sports and activities, cycling is best enjoyed as part of a group or team. Joining a club of like-minded people that share your passion for cycling will enhance your knowledge and enjoyment of it, giving you the opportunity to explore new territory and also you'll benefit from the 'team spirit' club riding is all about. Also your club companions can give you much needed support, advice and encouragement when the going gets tough. Embarking on race days and group days out can offer an extra dimension that riding solo does not provide.

How to find a club

One of the best ways of finding a local cycling club is the Internet. Online you'll find a wealth of information about clubs near and far, their history, their fees and what they have to offer. You can access them either by using a search engine or by visiting sites such as British Cycling and the CTC. The CTC site is particularly useful as it gives details on events held nationwide, plus contact information for district associations. See the help list for contact details of these and other cycling organisations and clubs.

Another way of finding local clubs is by word of mouth. Personal recommendations are valuable and reliable sources of information about how good an organisation or club is. Also if the recommendation comes from a

'Once you have started to see some gains, then you can graduate to higher intensity workouts both on and off of the bike.'

current member of the club you'll avoid the daunting task of joining as a total stranger, instead at least one person will be familiar, keeping you from feeling too self-conscious at the first meeting or practice session. The shop where you purchased either your bike or any of your cycle accessories may be another good place to ask as it is likely that they will have some information about local activities and clubs.

The road to glory?

At first, the club you join may offer you all you thought you wanted from it: mutual interest and companionship – but in time you may want more. The temptation to move away from 'hobby' cycling and into the exciting world of competitive cycling may prove to be too much, and you may find yourself longing to be on the starting line of racing event. Again, this is where the advice and encouragement of your club companions can be invaluable, helping to prepare you for what can be a nerve-wracking first outing on the competitive circuit. Having said that, you will find this element of the sport very different, as you will be racing under team orders and the interests of your teammates may sometimes have be considered above your own.

For this and other reasons, competitive cycling is not for everyone; but the great thing about being part of a cycling club is that if you do try it and decide it's not for you, simply change direction and take part in activities that are more suited to you and your goals.

Cycling clubs are established to promote the enjoyment and availability of the sport. They are always looking to increase their numbers by attracting newcomers, meaning their approach is welcoming, friendly and helpful. You may find the odd person who is too competitive and takes it too seriously, but rest assured most clubs are happy to invite beginners into their midst, and set them on the road to cycling success.

Summing Up

■ Making progress is a steady process of increasing time riding at each workout and also how many times per week.

■ Changing terrains and building endurance makes a difference in overall performance.

■ Joining a cycling club can offer many benefits for the new rider and seasoned riders.

Chapter 8

Going the Distance:
Time Trial Racing

What is a time trial?

A time trial is a race against the clock. Riders start a minute apart and you are racing on your own against the clock and yourself. Most events are 10, 25, 50 or 100 miles, but they are fixed distances. There are also fixed time events that are 12 and 24 hours. During those, you ride as far as you can in that time frame. Courses are generally on public roads and are either an out and back or they will use a roundabout as a halfway point or they may have a circuit feel with all left turns. You probably will need to be a member of a cycling club to participate in a time trial.

Why do a time trial?

This is a way to learn what your limits are and to give you a sense of productivity because you have accomplished something that required an all or nothing push to do. In time trials, slower riders set off first so the times tend to cluster at the end anyway, so don't feel as though you are unable to do one because you are new to the sport or are too slow. You will get a personal best time and then you can build on that for a second one and so on. Remember you are racing yourself, so no one else's time is important.

Where do you ride?

Public roads and measured courses are the time trial tracks. Make sure that you follow the rules of the road even in a time trial because the traffic won't know that you are racing against the clock.

A time trial starts with a group of cyclists ready to ride. Small markings on curbs and on the road can give the riders directions along the way. Sometimes there are signs that warn a cycling race is in progress, but often you are just riding along on a street with people going about their days or evenings. Look into joining the fun, most cycling clubs are happy to welcome newcomers.

How to race

If time trials are the most exciting event for you, then joining a club that is affiliated with cycling time trials is for you. That way you can ride in any of the events that are offered, instead of only the ones that are local to you. There may be an annual membership to belong to this as well as your club fees, but it should be affordable.

If a time trial is classified as an open event, then you must register in advance and there may be a fee that is higher than a club-only event. Sometimes, there are time trials that are a try-out event. Anyone can come and see if the club is for them during one of these events.

Time trial tip

A tip is to be as low as you can on the bike, so adjust your handlebars down a bit and wear clothing that is fitted. Since you are the biggest air resistance on your bike, anything that cuts down on the drag is important. This can help your time in addition to your overall fitness level.

Preparing properly

Equipment

A road-ready bike that can be a mountain bike or a touring one is the basic requirement. Add a helmet and you are off. Buying a starter bike like a Specialized Allez or a Trek 1000 can be sufficient and you can use it for training if you buy a better model for racing after some time.

Training

For a first time trial no training is needed except a basic level of cycling fitness. Attempt to go really fast for several miles and see how it feels before a trial and check that your riding position will work when riding at top speed.

Practise with more frequent rides and not more intense ones, and know that training will make a difference over weeks and not days.

'Changing up a gear' training can be done by picking a landmark ahead and riding towards it. Sprint if it is close and just go hard if it is a half mile or more away. Then once you reach it, ease off and pick a new one to do the same thing. Just make sure that you have the time for your body to recover before the event, so don't do any hard rides a few days before it.

On the day

Don't race on a full stomach. Have a banana three or four hours before the event and be sure to drink plenty of water.

Arrive early to get settled and to register and get your number to safety pin to your jersey. If you have the time, go down the road a bit to warm up. Get to the start with a few minutes to spare. Clip into the pedals – and you're off! Find a rhythm that is hard but sustainable at the beginning. Don't let your mind wander and don't worry about other riders passing you. When you see the finish line, give it all you've got. After, have a drink and wait for the timekeeper to let you know your time.

During the race

Use some basic strategy and understand some dos and don'ts that might make the race smoother. Don't be intimidated by the well-equipped and experienced riders, you don't have to have all the gadgets to ride well.

Simple strategy

- Pick your place – If it is your first time racing in a group, then pick an appropriate spot to get comfortable in the race without charging right out of the gate.
- Keep your head up, not on the rear wheel of the person in front.
- Consider your fitness – avoid exhaustion by racing smart for yourself.
- Try not to be at the back of the group to avoid hazards and the accordion effect of the pack.

Size up your competition

- Take notice of your competition – this is important if you are racing without a team. Teams working together can gain an advantage. Pay attention to them and be ready to capitalise on any mistakes they may make.
- Resist the urge to chase down every attack – make it count.

'If you race smart, you don't always need to be the strongest – racing as much with your head as your legs will greatly increase your chances at getting across the line first.'

If you race smart, you don't always need to be the strongest – racing as much with your head as your legs will greatly increase your chances at getting across the line first.

Bottle-handling skills

- Practise drinking from your bottle on training rides so you don't drop it during a race.
- A dropped bottle can cause others to fall and bicycle damage – be careful.

Be tough-skinned

- Ignore the egos.

Need2Know

- Let the legs do the talking and not the mouths.
- Just ride your own race.

Always a reason

- If the race doesn't go as planned, then just chalk it up to a bad day and move on, don't blame something/someone for it.

Use style to your advantage

- Close shave – smooth legs make less drag.
- Fashionably fast – tuck gel packs in the legs of your shorts.
- Glasses, straps, and sunglass earpieces should be on the outside of the helmet. Place your water bottle on the bike and not on your back.

You're just a number

- The right placement is key. Match the other riders for placement and make sure your number is not upside down.
- Ask someone to put it on if you think you will put it on crooked.

Sinus-clearing technique

- Please move off the side if you need to clear your nose. It may be running from the adrenaline and temperature, but the riders behind you don't want a shower, so moving aside will be appreciated.

Setting goals

Dream

- Brainstorm – What brings you joy? What energises you? Makes you excited about life?

Research

* Determine what events are coming up locally and even some that have travel opportunities or ones you could volunteer in.

Ask around

* Don't be influenced by others, but maybe ask what they think you should do or try.

Dig deep

* Find how your goal ties into your dreams and purpose in life. Tie your goal to your overall dream and purpose in life.

Define

'Make your goal specific, measurable, achievable and realistic.'

* Write it down right away to solidify your commitment to the goal.

* Make your goal specific, measurable, achievable and realistic. You need to be clear about what it is you are striving for, how you know you are getting to it and that you are able to achieve it. If the goal isn't realistic, then it may seem unattainable.

An example of a specific goal is: 'I will ride my bike or run 3 days per week for at least 30 minutes each day to build my cardiovascular endurance, and will sign up with my personal trainer to do resistance training twice a week to build lean muscle. Doing both of these will increase my overall fitness and enable me to have more energy throughout my day and for my family.'

Time-sensitive

* A timeline and maybe a date that you will accomplish your goal by can help make it seem possible.

Plan rewards and checkpoints

* Little rewards along the way keep you motivated and on track.

* Keep tabs on your progress to make sure that you are on schedule.

Do it

※ Get started on making your goals a reality today! No more excuses.

※ Join a group or have friends or family help you through any bumps along the way.

If your goal has to do with being more active, then riding in your first bike race or hitting a new personal best in a time trial might be a good way to achieve your goal.

Food and drink

※ Eat a diet high in carbohydrates and low in fat for the best endurance performance.

※ Water has no calories, but it is important to an athlete's performance. In cycling, rapid skin evaporation means that you will feel the perspiration less and so the fluid loss can be underestimated.

※ Fluid loss may exceed a litre per hour. Start off adequately hydrated, begin fluid replacement early, and drink regularly during the ride.

※ Weigh yourself before the ride and after. If there's a loss of a pound or two you are okay, but if there is more then you may need to rethink your training regimen.

※ Chocolate milk might be an option if you are looking for a complex carbohydrate drink.

Fatigue

A cyclist may experience 4 distinct types of fatigue.

※ The bonk (fatigue resulting from muscle glycogen depletion) can develop one to two hours into a ride.

※ Post-ride fatigue is the good tired; it is a normal response to several hours of vigorous exercise. Push training limits in a productive way that leads to improved performance the next time out.

- Over-reaching is the fatigue at the end of a hard week of riding. With recovery it can make us faster and stronger.

- Overtraining is the overwhelming and often long-term (lasting weeks to months) fatigue. This type is limiting rather than stimulating improvement to performance.

As a regular course of events, a rider should assess his or her level of post-ride fatigue. To minimise the risk of overtraining, you should include at least one, and occasionally two, rest days per week along with a day of easy spinning.

Over-reaching is a normal part of the training cycle. It may require recovery days. Your performance should be improving with several extra recovery days, but if not, then it's time to take a break from riding.

Don't risk overtraining which may require a month or two off the bike to recover.

Summing Up

- Choose the right distance if you are going to race.
- Try a time trial to see if you are interested in that kind of riding.
- Prepare for the race and don't be intimidated by more experienced riders.
- Make your goal specific, measurable, achievable and realistic.
- Hydrate before, during and after a race or training exercise.
- Measure and evaluate fatigue for the best results for your performance.

Chapter 9

Enjoy the Ride

Your cycling routine

Changing the routine

Changing your workout routine is important because the same routine may not yield the best results. By altering the routine, things may be more interesting and it may serve as more motivation for you. It's also a great thing to do if you are looking to lose weight, as muscle confusion and routine change-up are proven ways to make your body work harder and shed the pounds quicker!

Why you should change your workout routine

Once you find exercises that work for you and that you like to do, you may see good results, but after a while you can become stagnant, and the weight loss or other fitness goals may be harder to maintain. This is because with the repetition of the same workout your body will consume less energy once it is accustomed to it. By changing the routine, your body is always challenged and it will burn more calories and result in more weight loss. People often quit due to boredom of the exercises, but this way you can keep it interesting if it is always changing. A change can be in intensity or the type of workout.

How often to change your workout routine

Some experts believe that a daily change is helpful, but even if you change once every two or four weeks, you will still probably see changes for the better.

How to change workout routines

If you want to change, you may have to be creative. Talk with your trainer or others to find out what they do for their routines. If you run, add more sprints, change routes or do intervals of other exercise in-between. Changing gym equipment can help, too. On the bikes, do a more intense ride by adding speed or sprints for some of the workout time.

Challenging your body on a regular basis by altering the routine will keep you burning calories efficiently and keep the laziness out of your workout.

Exploring new terrain

While not everyone gets to cycle in faraway, exotic locations, it is a nice way to tour the world and one that affirms that cycling is a worldwide exercise and enjoyment. You are in good company, indeed. Here are a few foreign locations to visit – many dedicated cyclists love to take a trip and travel with their bikes. Do yourself a favour and discover a new part of the world while enjoying all the benefits of cycling!

Rolling vineyards, Piedmont, Italy

The foot of the Italian Alps is ideal for exploring by bike. There is a new self-guided hotel-to-hotel cycling trip available and it also adds stops for tastings and meals. Every night or two you stay in a different hotel along the way. Enjoy the local sights as you go.

Downhill mountain biking, Austria

Can you imagine spending a week in the Austrian Alps? You could go to the 4,500m-long downhill track on Planai mountain. You'll explore three different resort areas: Schladming, Wagrain and Leogang on this trip. With demanding terrain, superb downhill tracks and facilities for the serious biker, this is a trip to be reckoned with. It does offer cable car rides to ease some of the climbs.

Sun and Cycling, Ionian Islands, Greece

On the Ionian Islands off the west coast of Greece, you will get a tan while cycling picturesque hills. The group will cycle 25-50km a day and will have stops at beaches and taverns. Relax on board the yacht that is your accommodation for the week.

Cobbles, Bikes and Beer, Belgium

A tough new challenge for road cyclists could be to try biking the Belgian way. Tackle the cobbles of Deinze, the Flemish town where Eddy Merckx honed his skills. Ride the long cobbled street from Kerkgate to Wolvenberg Hill, part of the Tour of Flanders: 1,100m of cobbled climbing and a maximum gradient of 20%. After doing various road rides and completing the final section of the Paris-Roubaix route, you can take a shower in the old Velodrome building, hit the brewery in Gavere and take in the Eddy Merckx Velodrome in Ghent for an introduction to track racing.

Canal Cruise, Amsterdam to Bruges

Take this slow, easy route from Amsterdam to Bruges via Antwerp and Ghent. Stay on a large canal barge, which operates as a moving base for seven days of easy, flat cycling, for a group of up to 24 people. You can choose to cycle as a group with a leader or independently to meet the barge again each night for a well-deserved dinner.

Find other cycling friends

Finding a cycling club that you can enjoy being a part of can keep you motivated, build and hone skills and help you to make friends. Some clubs are geared towards road biking, BMX or mountain biking and others are strictly about racing. A little research can unearth all the choices in your area. See the help list for details of UK cycling clubs. Once you are a part of the cycling club then you will have opportunities to socialise as well as ride. During the winter, many clubs organise demonstrations and speakers to keep people motivated and in contact, even when the snow falls.

Seven ways to stay motivated for cycling in winter

1 – Set goals. Write them down and also share them with others so you have the support to actually achieve the goals. Be realistic and build in milestones that you can accomplish on your way to finishing. That way you can feel the goal is attainable.

2 – Sign up for a ride. Make sure that you train for the ride and have properly registered before showing up.

3 – Do a fundraiser. Cycling for a worthy cause is always an option. Help for Heroes charity bike ride and the Doitforcharity Three Cities Cycle Ride are some events in 2013 that offer cyclists a chance to participate in a fun riding experience for a good cause.

4 – Challenge a friend. Remember to keep the rivalry friendly, but this can be a great motivator.

5 – Join a cycle club or join a regular group ride. There are many cycle clubs that can provide inspiration as well as a great way to make new friends. If you look, there will be someone who is in similar condition to you and can help you push even harder towards your goals. It is also the perfect way to socialise and make cycling fun and enjoyable.

6 – Wear proper clothes for the weather. No numb fingers and toes are allowed, so make warm removable layers of clothing your priority and remember to hydrate.

7 – Reward yourself. Choose a personal motivator that you enjoy as a reward for remaining motivated. It can be something simple, like a night of total relaxation or something with a bigger price tag like a bike accessory. The important thing is to celebrate your accomplishments so that there is motivation to make more progress.

Keeping focused on your goal is important, but recognising the process of getting there is also important because each step takes work and effort. Staying fit and healthy when you are not able to be cycling all the time is not easy, but it is possible.

Sticking with it

Losing motivation for whatever reason happens to everyone, even the most dedicated cyclists. One reason to lose motivation is if you get sick or if you have pain that makes cycling difficult or impossible for any length of time. Sometimes aches and pains and even minor illnesses can be caused by overtraining. Taking a week or so off may not be a bad thing because you will want to go back at the end, but if you slug through feeling bad and unmotivated, then you can struggle more and even give up on cycling altogether.

- Less is more. Keep your cycling fun and reduce the amount that you train and enjoy the rest days as much as the training. As mentioned in a previous chapter, prioritise high-intensity workout days rather than recovery rides or slow longer rides.

- Build in a pleasure day on the bike. Enjoy a gentle ride and enjoy the scenery and hopefully sunshine.

- Remember why you took up cycling. Whether it was to improve your fitness, lose weight, or to simply have fun. Staying in touch with those reasons can make it easier to stay motivated.

- Training focuses on aspects of your cycling which need a little work, but this can make you feel like there is only negativity about cycling. Change or add aspects that you like and enjoy when you are training so that you won't lose motivation. A day off from incline climbing for a flat route with pretty scenery won't hurt anything.

- Enjoy a training session with a friend. Cycling with people can help you identify strengths and weaknesses and can offer friendly competition that can do wonders for motivation.

It is important to find a level that encourages you to continue riding, not a level that exhausts and discourages you.

'Remember why you took up cycling. Whether it was to improve your fitness, lose weight, or to simply have fun. Staying in touch with those reasons can make it easier to stay motivated.'

Helping yourself and celebrating successes

- Have you been trying and failing to lose weight? If you don't enjoy the process, then you may be struggling more. When you are discouraged, you will eat more things that should be your special treats. Being positive and enjoying the process is very important to the success.

- Set small goals with rewards. Make sure that these goals are attainable and that you are not setting yourself up to fail.

- Celebrate the small achievements. For instance, if you want to lose twenty pounds, reward yourself for every five pounds lost.

- Track your progress. Use your Android or iPhone or other fitness device to help you along the way, in addition to your scale.

- Make it a group effort. Find a weight loss buddy in your circle of friends or recruit a family member or start your own club for weight loss. Exercising with a group of friends can be more fun than on your own.

- Forgive yourself. Don't be too hard on yourself. Look ahead and praise yourself for the good work that you've already done.

- Give yourself permission to take a break or indulge every once in a while.

- Remember that weight loss is a lifestyle change. You want and need to be healthier. All things in moderation is key. Figure out what works the best for you and go with it.

- Reward yourself. Your dedicated efforts deserve to be rewarded. With the celebration, you adopt a positive attitude and this positive outlook will have you hopping out of bed and putting a pep in your step.

Summing Up

- Changing a workout routine is a great way to stay motivated, keep the calories burning and keep boredom out of the routine.

- Exploring new terrain can help to motivate you and to offer different challenges for training.

- Cycling clubs help you to practise skills, learn new techniques and to make friends who share your love for cycling.

- Staying fit during the off times can be a challenge. Keep your motivation high by varying the workouts, setting goals and doing other exercises.

- Find ways to stay motivated so you don't give up on cycling if you hit a rough patch in training.

- Celebrate your successes in small ways and in bigger tangible rewards.

- Have fun doing what you love – which by now should be cycling!

Glossary

Bicycle
A non-motorised vehicle with two wheels, using pedals connected to the back wheel to propel itself. Also features handlebars and a saddle.

Cadence
Ideal rhythm. In cycling, your cadence will be the speed you are cycling at, similar to a pace.

Cross-country
A type of race or riding that takes place over fields and through woods rather than on a beaten path or determined road.

Cross training
Supplementing a main workout activity with other activities that may work various muscles neglected during the main workout. Cross training can also benefit the main workout by working out similar muscles or recreating similar movements while involving different activities.

Cycling
The act of riding a bicycle. Cycling can also refer to the bike race in itself.

Cyclist
The individual riding a bicycle, and enjoying the act of cycling. Can be amateur or professional.

Drafting
Drafting is a technique cyclists use where they cycle in single file so the person at the front blocks the wind for the people behind. They take it in turns to be the rider at the front.

Endurance
The ability, or capacity, to endure something through difficult conditions. In cycling, your endurance could be defined by your ability to manage hills consistently despite fatigue or adverse conditions, for example. A cyclist with good endurance can train longer and is usually more competitive.

Fatigue

A weariness of your body or mental state. Cyclists are very prone to fatigue if they forget to eat and sleep properly and take care of their body between high-intensity workout sessions, for example.

Overtraining

To overdo something, such as your training. Cyclists need to plan their training carefully in order to get enough workout sessions but still not overtrain for a particular event or race.

Paceline riding

The act of riding in a group. If you have joined a cycling group or tend to go riding with a few people, you'll be paceline riding.

Peloton

The main field or group of cyclists in a race.

Reflector

Something that reflects. Cyclists will usually wear reflector vests, or equip their bike with various small reflectors to be seen by motorists while they are riding in darker hours.

Spinning

A type of indoor cycling, usually done in groups or classes, which focuses on endurance, strength and interval training. Spinning is known to be a very high-intensity workout.

Help List

Cycling clubs

British Cycling

www.britishcycling.org.uk
Telephone: 0161 274 2000
Fax: 0161 274 2001
Email: info@britishcycling.org.uk
British Cycling is the national governing body for cycling.
British Cycling and the Great Britain Cycling Team receive many requests to support charity events and individual fundraising challenges.

CTC (The National Cycling Charity)

www.ctc.org.uk
Telephone: 0844 736 8450
Whether you're new to cycling, ride regularly or want to get back into it, we cater for you. With over 130 years' experience to share, we are passionate about helping more people to enjoy the benefits of cycling.

Newbury Road Club

www.newburyrc.co.uk
Chairman (Ian Greenstreet)
Telephone: 07770 220080
Newbury Road Club serves cyclists in the Newbury (Berkshire, UK) catchment area, approximately 60 miles west of London on the M4 corridor. It has been established since 1925. Whilst it promotes all forms of cycling it is primarily a road club supporting in particular all forms of on-road riding. In 2010 the club celebrated its 85th anniversary.
Our membership numbers between 100 and 200, and encompasses the whole spectrum of age with active members of all ages, women, men, boys and girls. We see our club as having an important function in promoting not

only competitive events but also in being a voice and a focus for cyclists in the Newbury area. The club has representation on the local authority West Berkshire Cycle Forum.

Peterborough Cycling Club

www.peterboroughcyclingclub.co.uk
Telephone: 07970 752077
The Peterborough Cycling Club is the oldest continuously active cycling club in the country. Although other clubs claim to have been founded at an earlier date, the Peterborough club is, to the best of our knowledge, the only one that has not ceased to exist at some point and then been reformed. Although the club badge shows 1874, latest research into the clubs history, has shown that it was actually founded in 1873.

Solihull Cycling Club

www.solihullcc.org.uk
Telephone: 01926 427200
Email: chair@solihullcc.org.uk
Welcome to the Solihull Cycling Club. Founded in 1929, the SCC is one of the most successful cycling clubs in the history of UK cycling.
The SCC is an extremely diverse cycling club which promotes all aspects of the sport. It is proud to have a racing heritage that has produced National Champions, Olympic Medallists, World Champions and Tour de France riders whilst at the same time, keeping the spirit of the club alive in non-racing and social activities.

The Tandem Club of the United Kingdom

www.tandem-club.org.uk
Email: tc@beam.ltd.uk
Full membership is available on an annual basis or on a commuted one for five years. Membership is available to anyone who rides regularly with a Full Member; at least one applicant must take out Full Membership. The first Joint Member is enrolled free. Family membership, which is also free, is open to all dependants of the Full Member aged 17 or under residing at the same address. There is a nominal charge for other Joint Members.

The Wollybacks Mountain Biking Club

www.thewollybacks.co.uk
Email: admin@thewoollybacks.co.uk
If you would like any further information about the club, the type of riding we do or to join the club please do not hesitate to contact us by email or log onto the forum and introduce yourself. We really are a friendly group who make newcomers very welcome.

Cycling resources

British Heart Foundation

www.bhf.org.uk
Telephone: 020 7554 0000
To help you pedal off on the right foot, we've got lots of fantastic tips and advice on training for your bike ride in our cycling zone.

Cycle Solutions

www.cyclesolutions.co.uk
Telephone: 0330 100 2480
A useful website where you will find information on purchasing bike helmets and their safety requirements.

Cycle Store.co.uk

www.cyclestore.co.uk
Telephone: 01260 275554
Great website with a huge range of products that caters to all cycling requirements. Also gives details of their trading shop based in Congleton, Cheshire.

Cycle World.co.uk

www.cycleworld.co.uk
Online bike shop selling a massive range of cycles and accessories from well-known manufacturers. They have shops located in the south of England in Portsmouth, Romsey and Southampton. They also offer bike servicing options.

Hooked On Cycling

www.hookedoncycling.co.uk
Company that sells and organises cycling holidays in exotic locations such as Greece, Italy, Austria and Belgium.

References

About.com Basic Nutrition for Better Bike Riding Eat Right - Fuel the Machine! From Tera Liescheidt, R.D. (online) http://bicycling.about.com/od/cyclingforabetterbody/a/nutrition_bikes.htm accessed on June 23, 2012

About.com Cross Training to Enhance Your Cycling Different Workouts Can Help You on the Bike By David Fiedler (online) http://bicycling.about.com/od/trainingandfitness/a/crosstrain.htm accessed on June 23, 2012

Active.com (online) June 10, 2010 http://www.active.com/gear/Articles/Beginner_s-Guide-to-Bike-Gear.htm accessed on June 23, 2012

Adult Bicycling.com (online) 2009http://www.adultbicycling.com/component/content/article/27-cycling-shoes.html accessed on June 24, 2012

A Guide to Trail Safety Trail Congestion is Causing Hazards Joel Hirschhorn (online)

Aug 31, 2006 http://voices.yahoo.com/a-guide-trail-safety-68744.html?cat=11 accessed on June 23, 2012 http://www.womenscycling.ca/blog/sheila-psychling/unofficial-rules-of-cycling-etiquette/

BBC News (online)

Bicycling.com Seven Steps to Better Cycling http://www.bicycling.com/training-nutrition/injury-prevention/7-steps-pain-free-cycling accessed on June 23, 2012

Confessions of a weight-loss cyclist (online)By Jane Elliott Health reporter, BBC News Saturday, 11 April 2009 http://news.bbc.co.uk/2/hi/health/7953197.stm accessed on June 23, 2012

Cycle helmets – an overview Last revised June 2012 http://www.cyclehelmets.org/1139.html accessed on June 23, 2012

Cycling Resource Centre May 2012 (online) http://www.cyclingresourcecentre.org.au/post/bicycle_wayfinding_for_metropolitan_melbourne accessed on June 23, 2012

Cyclists Touring Club (CTC) (online) available at: http://www.ctc.org.uk/desktopdefault.aspx?tabid=3789 accessed on June 23, 2012.

Fit Day Beta (online) The Proper Bike Gear: What to Wear and When?http://www.fitday.com/fitness-articles/fitness/equipment/the-proper-bike-gear-what-to-wear-and-when.html accessed on June 23, 2012.

Harris Cyclery A Comfortable Saddle (online) http://sheldonbrown.com/saddles.html accessed on June 23, 2012

Joe to Pro Cycling Sleep and become a stronger cyclist December 13, 2011 (online) http://joetoprocycling.com/sleep-and-become-a-stronger-cyclist/ accessed on June 23, 2012 Livestrong.com Cycling and Sore Elbows Jun 14, 2011 (online) By Dan Harrimanhttp://www.livestrong.com/article/470814-cycling-elbow-soreness/ accessed on June 24, 2012

Livestrong.com Cycling and Sore Feet Mar 9, 2011 (online) By Shannon Marks http://www.livestrong.com/article/399954-cycling-sore-feet/ accessed on June 24, 2012

Livestrong.com GENERAL SAFETY RULES WHEN RIDING BICYCLES (online) Mar 7, 2011 By Toby Pendergrasshttp://www.livestrong.com/article/398464-general-safety-rules-when-riding-bicycles/ accessed on June 23, 2012

Livestrong.com (online) Mar 28, 2011 Stationary Bike Benefits, by Debby Maynes available at: http://www.livestrong.com/article/81995-stationary-bike-benefits/ accessed on June 23, 2012.

Livestrong.com (online) Jun 3, 2010 What are the Benefits of a Tandem Bicycle? By Rob Callahan http://www.livestrong.com/article/138980-what-are-benefits-tandem-bicycle/ accessed on June 23, 2012.

The loneliness of the long distance cyclist June 12, 2010 (online) Collette Freedman http://colettefreedman.com/2012/06/the-loneliness-of-the-distance-cyclist/ accessed on June 24, 2012

Mayo Clinic (online) http://www.mayoclinic.com/health/bicycle-helmet/HQ00324/NSECTIONGROUP=2 accessed on June 24, 2012.

Roadbike Review.com 10 Tips to Avoid Looking Like a Rookie December 9, 2008 (online) http://reviews.roadbikereview.com/10-tips-to-avoid-looking-like-a-cycling-rookie accessed on June 24, 2012

Sporty Afros Workout Confession: My Lack of Motivation To Workout (online) http://sportyafros.com/all-about-alexandria/workout-confession-my-lack-of-motivation-for-working-out/ accessed on June 23, 2012

Team Estrogen.com (online) http://www.teamestrogen.com/content/beginnerCyclist accessed on June 23, 2012

Training for Cyclists.com (online) http://www.training4cyclists.com/ accessed on June 23, 2012

Unofficial Rules of Cycling Etiquette By Sheila Ascroft http://www.dailypeloton.com/gstepan.asp accessed on June 23, 2012

Web MD Fitness Basics are Back By Barbara Russi Sarnataro WebMD Weight Loss Clinic-Feature Reviewed by Louise Chang, MDhttp://www.webmd.com/fitness-exercise/guide/fitness-basics-exercise-bike-is-back accessed on June 24, 2012

WNDU.com (available online) http://www.wndu.com/mmm/headlines/7731007.html accessed on June 24, 2012

Web MD Fitness Basics are Back By Barbara Russi Sarnataro WebMD Weight Loss Clinic-Feature Reviewed by Louise Chang, MDhttp://www.webmd.com/fitness-exercise/guide/fitness-basics-exercise-bike-is-back accessed on June 24, 2012

WNDU.com (available online) http://www.wndu.com/mmm/headlines/7731007.html accessed on June 24, 2012

Yahoo! Voices.com

Yahoo! Voices.com A Guide to Correct Bicycle Road Etiquette Sophie Spyrou, Sep 18, 2008 (online) http://voices.yahoo.com/a-guide-correct-bicycle-road-etiquette-1911212.html?cat=27 accessed on June 23, 2012

Zen Habits Beginner's Guide to Cycling (online) http://zenhabits.net/beginners-guide-to-cycling/ accessed on June 23, 2012

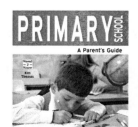

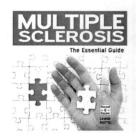